Survive and Thrive on the Witness Stand

A 15 Step Guide

by Dr. Michael S. Alexander

Printed in the United States of America

ISBN-13: 978-1975682330

ISBN-10: 1975682335

Alexander Talks
45 East Rodell Place
Arcadia, CA 91006
<Michael@AlexanderTalks.com>

http://www.AlexanderTalks.com

ACKNOWLEDGEMENTS

Cover Design by Christina Hamlett

Coverage Image: Wikimedia Commons

http://www.AlexanderTalks.com

Table of Contents

http://www.AlexanderTalks.com

Introduction

There are a number of reasons why someone might find themselves on the witness stand:

- Criminal Cases
- Civil Cases
- Contract Disputes
- Discrimination Suits
- Wrongful Dismissal Suits
- Regulatory Proceedings
- State and Federal Congressional Investigations
- Divorce
- Custody Hearings

This book is intended for the people who are—or who will soon be—witnesses, lawyers who need to know how to train and support their own witnesses, and anyone curious about how the whole process works. When you finish, you should have a better idea of what being a witness is actually like, how to prepare yourself, how to anticipate the questions which you might be asked, and how to respond to both the questions you expected and those you did not.

It doesn't matter whether you are a professional witness or a bystander who happened to observe something. It doesn't matter if you are only testifying out of a sense of right and wrong or if you are the defendant (or plaintiff) yourself. The basic techniques, problems, and things to look out for are the same.

My Background

I've spent over 25 years as an expert witness and have provided written and oral testimony in over 175 cases. It is a job I love and, for me, it is a lot of fun. My family has been involved in theatre for generations, I love a good argument, and—being a game player by nature—I have all of the advantages to make being a witness comfortable and fun. I also trained many others, colleagues and students to be witnesses, including coaching an award-winning mock trial team of middle school students.

It would be a mistake, though to assume that when I started as a witness I could just sit down on the witness stand without learning the necessary skills.

It would also be a mistake to assume you cannot learn them yourself. You can, and this book will help you.

It didn't matter if I was appearing as an energy economist, defending myself during my divorce, or prepping others to sit in the witness stand. I thought of being a witness as a game, not as serious a game as professional football, but nevertheless as a game. Those who do it with the right attitude and the right training/preparation do it well and with a lot less stress than those who do not.

Being a game does not make it trivial. It does not mean you can "win" without preparation and training, without understanding the rules, or without understanding the other side's strategy. These are all important. Again, consider a professional football game. The players spend months training, scouting and learning the strategies, strengths and weaknesses of the other teams they play. They also learn a lot about the rules, how to stop the clock or keep it running, when to call a time-out, and when to save that time-out for later. A good attitude, like a good pep talk, helps but it isn't everything.

My first appearance on the witness stand was as a witness for the state in a natural gas rate case in Minnesota. Before they put me on the stand, our lawyers wanted to make sure I was ready. I wasn't nervous, but they wanted to make sure about a lot more than just stage fright. So they put ran me through a practice cross-examination.

They were merciless. For almost an hour, they grilled and challenged my background, my credentials, my inexperience, my data, my analysis, and my motivations. Their goal was *not* to make me less afraid to be on the witness stand; it was to terrify me into taking the whole procedure seriously. Part of their procedure was simply to batter me down. They had a lot of stamina because they had been in long trials and proceedings. They figured I would be exhausted from the constant battering. But before it was over, they, too, had begun to sweat.

"Wow," they said at last. "That was pretty impressive. We couldn't break you. You stood fast, had counter-arguments which were solid and didn't say anything you shouldn't have. That was one of the most powerful performances we've ever seen. Just don't ever do it again!"

I had been strong and aggressive. I fought back at every question. I was also comfortable doing it, although I was burning a lot of adrenaline. The problem, though, was that I was not likable and, therefore, I was not winning over my audience. Success required that the judge believe I was an expert, not just that I was a "fighter." And I was not helping my lawyers. They didn't know how to defend me if I got into trouble. In fact, since this was a technical proceeding, they didn't know enough to follow everything at all. Further, I wasn't necessarily making the points they wanted to make in their legal briefs (summation), so I was not necessarily helping the cause. *I* was doing well, but only for myself. I wasn't helping the case.

Looking at me and my style, they suggested a different approach. They wanted me to be more professorial. "We can't actually tell you to wear a tweed jacket with leather patches, but that is the vibe you should be giving off." They then proceeded to talk about the points they needed to have me make in order to make our case.

I listened to them. I changed my style and it made me a much more effective witness and created a chance for me to work on negotiations outside of the courtroom. It also made the whole experience much more pleasant. As an even more important result, I am often favorably quoted in the judge's final decisions which is, after all, the true measure of my success as a witness.

Way back in high school, one of my buddies signed my yearbook, "To the only person I enjoy losing an argument to." Of all of the lines that all of my friends signed in that yearbook, no other was quite as insightful. Yes, I enjoyed argument and debate. I loved taking a different side than others. Still, it was always a game for me, an intellectual exercise, and I always felt it should be fun for the other person as well. If I were to describe the ideal mindset for a professional witness, that would be it. If I am making sure I am likable while I am arguing a side, the favorable impression I make on the judge will pay off.

A Proper Mindset For The Witness Stand

There are two things people are typically told when they are going to be on the witness stand:

- Just tell the truth and everything will be fine.
- Say as little as possible.

Just tell the truth and everything will be fine

Telling the truth is good advice. Expecting everything to "be fine" is a good way to get blindsided! It isn't nearly that simple. I am a strong advocate of telling the truth both from a moral point of view and from a practical one. The odds of being caught in a lie are high, and the consequences are very unpleasant. However, the opposing lawyers are trained to find the weaknesses in your story or make what was logical and real sound far-fetched and unbelievable. True, for the most part, the "disagreements" in any proceeding are "legitimate differences of opinion between men of good will" and the court is supposed to address them as such. But it is certainly possible to tell the truth without being convincing (just as there are convincing liars). Remember, it isn't just a matter of telling the truth: it is much more importantly a matter of getting the judge and jury to believe you.

Say as little as possible

There is much to be said for this advice. The less you say, the less chance there is that you will say something wrong. Indeed, the opposing lawyer's most potent weapon is the awkward silence. People often want to be helpful and, being uncomfortable with silence, they will say something, anything to end it, which often means they say something they shouldn't.

If you don't say anything, however, you don't strengthen your side's case either. The court will make a decision based on what people say in testimony. Thus, if you don't mention something important, it won't help your case.

The important "trick" is to say all of the right things, and none of the wrong ones. But, also to *make sure you say it in the most believable way possible*. This book is intended to help you do just that.

1. Understand That Legal Proceedings In The Courtroom Are Theatre

What happens in a courtroom is not as simple as lawyers trying to get at the truth with the help of the witnesses. What happens in a courtroom is theatre. The lawyers are trying to present a story with the help of the witnesses. Ultimately, a courtroom decision is based on how good a story each side tells and how well they tell it.

Being a good witness, therefore, means knowing how to present yourself and your story. You cannot just go up on the witness stand with all of the facts and expect the court's decision to go your way. To be a good witness, you need to think about how the information you are giving will be perceived by "the audience." And you need to tell it like a story. The facts have to be developed and presented in such a way that they flow and so that the judge and jury can understand, become involved in, and "feel" the truth in that story. Remember that while you do not want to insult their intelligence, you also should not assume they will fill in any details the way you would, no matter how obvious those details may seem to you.

It is important to remember that how you look, the language you use and the professionalism of your presentation all matter. Frankly, so does how likable you are.

Does appearance matter? Definitely! If you are a student appearing for a traffic violation, you might want to look a little naïve. For instance, you might want to wear slacks and a jacket with a tie that doesn't quite match. This will give you the appearance of trying but will play down the idea you are sophisticated and should have known what you were doing.

On the other hand, if you are appearing as a professional witness, you must also look the part. I was in one proceeding where the witness was a young, attractive blond with curly hair and bright lipstick. She looked like a college girl and, worse, she looked like a ditsy blond. Forgive the stereotype, but if people are affected by it, then they are affected by it whether it *should* matter or not.) One woman I know showed up to a custody hearing in a blouse that was too tight and showed a lot of cleavage. It did not help her case. A divorce attorney I know told me that getting her clients to dress conservatively in custody cases was a problem she had to deal with far more often than she would have believed … and it wasn't even a subject they taught her in law school.

Similarly, your attitude matters. In the Watergate Conspiracy trials, the prosecution was concerned they did not have a strong enough case against Robert Mardian, the lawyer for the Committee for the Re-Election of the President (and, in fact, his conviction was overturned on appeal). However, Mardian was so abrasive that the jury disliked him and, therefore, did not give him any benefit of the doubt. Accordingly, they convicted him of conspiracy.

Something similar happened in a case I worked on involving market manipulation. In that case there was a witness whose facts and analyses were completely overshadowed by his arrogant nature. He kept using phrases like "obviously" and "as any intelligent person could see." I found myself instinctively looking for reasons he was wrong … and I was on the same side as he was. The look on the judge's face made it clear the judge wasn't sympathetic to the witness, either. While the judge did not argue with the witness, none of the witness' testimony got more than the briefest passing mention when the judge wrote his decision. Regardless of how good a job of analysis the witness might have done, the witness' testimony carried no weight with the judge and did not affect the decision.

As an expert witness myself, I tend to play the role of the academic. I am charming and amusing (but not too much of either), and am always willing to explain everything in detail like a "beloved college professor." It gives me a lot of credibility and gets me quoted frequently in the judge's decisions, which is exactly what I am going for. The more I am quoted, the more the judge has accepted my arguments as legitimate. I make it easy for him to quote me by being clear and quotable. That helps what I say stick in his mind and it makes it easy to work my arguments into his decisions.

My grandfather used to tell a story of the time he was accused of taking a $25 bribe at the end of WWII to terminate a contract in favor of a particular munitions supplier. My grandfather went into court and opened with, "Your honor, I am insulted. Not at the accusation that I would take a bribe. If it were large enough, who can say if I would be tempted? But to be accused of being stupid enough to compromise my integrity and take the legal risk for a mere $25…"

The judge held up his hand, "You can stop right there. I always urge lawyers not to over-prosecute or over-defend their case. Case dismissed."

What my grandfather had done was to change the story from a story of a man who took a bribe to a story of a man who was stupid enough to risk everything for a trivial amount of money. That change took the case from being a difficult one to one that was so obvious the judge didn't feel a need to hear anything more to make a decision. Nonetheless, you have to be very careful in a situation like this. If you come off like a smart aleck, you will lose credibility and that definitely is not what you want to do.

NOTES ON THE COURTROOM AS THEATRE

_____

_____

_____

_____

_____

_____

_____

_____

_____

_____

_____

_____

_____

NOTES ON THE COURTROOM AS THEATRE (cont)

2.   Work With Your Lawyer

There are sports heroes but they do not act alone. Even the best quarterback has ten other guys on the field at all times. Golf has a reputation as a solo game, but a good caddy is worth his weight in gold and even Tiger Woods has a "swing coach."

The same is true in politics. Presidents have cabinets, and candidates have campaign staff. In entertainment, movies have multiple actors, stunt men, directors, cameramen, etc. Singers work with (at a minimum) a backup band.

Legal proceedings are no different. You and your lawyer are a team. He has been trained for courtroom situations—what the judge will actually accept as evidence and what will "ring true" with the jury. He also probably has a good idea of what will distract (or annoy) the judge and jury. Let him "direct" the action. On the other hand, he can't actually testify to anything (although he can either amuse or annoy a judge if he tries to). Court decisions must be decided based on what witnesses say in sworn testimony.

Therefore, you should work with your lawyer as a team. Make sure he knows and understands everything you have to say (or might want not to say). And make sure you know what points he wants you to make for him. And if you are uncomfortable with any of them, make sure he knows that you are uncomfortable and why. Also, work out a style and an approach with him. Remember that no lawyer likes to be surprised … ever!

One of my acquaintances told me a story of a case in which a janitor fell from a ladder at work, seriously injuring himself to such an extent he could not work again. His lawyer was hoping not just to get him workers' compensation for having been injured on the job, but also to get a settlement against the manufacturers of the ladder for the manufacture of an unsafe product. When the disabled janitor went on the stand, the lawyer asked him to describe what had happened. The janitor described the incident as an "accident."

The trouble with the word "accident" in this case is that it didn't cast any blame on the manufacturer of the ladder. The lawyer couldn't put words in his client's mouth so he said "Could you describe it another way?" hoping the witness would say something like, "When the ladder collapsed" (or better yet, "failed").

Alas for the witness, he did not get the hint. So, he again described it as an "accident." Although the lawyer tried again to suggest that another way of describing it would be helpful, the witness (who was in pain and nervous, not being used to being on the witness stand) did not have another way of describing it at his fingertips. He again said, "Accident. I don't know how else to describe it, that is what it was."

The disabled janitor did get a workers' compensation settlement, but since he had not said anything which implicated the ladder manufacture for faulty design (and, therefore, there was nothing on the record to implicate the manufacturer), he did not get any additional compensation from said ladder manufacturer. However, had the client and lawyer sat down and discussed the testimony in advance and the importance of saying the ladder "failed" or was otherwise "faulty," the manufacturer might have been found liable and there might have been an additional hefty settlement.

The first thing I do after I have read the facts of the case is to talk with my lawyer. We go over the facts of the case, what I know, what questions we might want to ask, the key points, etc. In many technical cases, I bring the lawyer up to speed on the key issues. As a professional, I have a series of PowerPoint slides I use to educate the lawyer; this helps him get up to speed and also cements any key ideas and concepts in my mind. We also discuss what the other side will try to "prove" and our responses. After that, I get to work on preparing my side of the case. When appearing as a witness, I often will help write questions for my lawyer to consider asking. He is the lawyer. I don't want to get in his way or waste his time, but I make suggestions that will help him inform him of the issues and then let him proceed from there.

Whether you want to or should go that far will depend upon your level of expertise in the subject area (expert witnesses should be more involved than others), and the number of issues you are dealing with out of the whole case. The point, however, is universal; specifically, work with your lawyer and understand your place in the proceeding so you can help, not just blindly follow the lawyers' leads (yours and the opposing lawyer's if you aren't careful).

Often, particularly in a case with a lot of technical details, a lawyer may choose to have another person (sometimes another lawyer, sometimes another expert witness) sit beside him to "ride shotgun." This second person has a number of functions. For instance, he may watch what the witness says for things which might create problems later. Did the witness say something that was not quite correct, was not clear, or which might be "twisted" by the opposing council later in the trial or in briefs (the summary of the case which the lawyers will ultimately present to the judge)? Is the witness getting tired or confused? How are the judge and jury reacting? Should the lawyer try to call a break so they can coach the witness accordingly?

When riding shotgun, I also work with my lawyer, especially on technical questions, to make sure they are aware of something the opposing side might have said that we either want to challenge, counter or use against them in the future. How much I can do that depends upon my experience with the rest of the case but, in some cases, we have multiple people riding shotgun, limiting their duties to the portions of the case they fundamentally understand. For some proceedings, I will sit by my lawyer's side throughout the entire case, making notes, whispering in the lawyer's ear, etc.

NOTES – WORK WITH YOUR LAWYER

NOTES – WORK WITH YOU LAWYER (cont)

_____

_____

_____

_____

_____

_____

_____

_____

_____

_____

_____

_____

_____

_____

_____

_____

_____

_____

3.   Always Tell The Truth And Don't Be Afraid To Say That You Don't Know Something

Never lie on the stand. This isn't just a matter of morality. If you say something that isn't true, you will be found out. Never underestimate your opponents.

In general, I try to understand as much of the case as possible, even things outside of my expertise, so I know what is or is not relevant. I want to know whether something I say will create a trap for another witness or if there is some extra light I can shed on an issue based on my expertise.

You should realize, however, I have a broad and eclectic background. I have been able to learn and pick up enough information to deal not just with energy cases (which is my primary area of expertise) but also with cases involving art forgery, arson, etc. Very few people have that kind of a background. More importantly, I know my limits. Never forget the phrase "a little knowledge is a dangerous thing." Never get out of your comfort zone or try to go past your level of competence. Remember that if you say something wrong, it can adversely affect your credibility even on stuff you have right. Saying "I don't know" is always better than saying the wrong thing.

Relax, you don't need to know everything. Even in my areas of expertise, I have frequently said, "I have not performed an analysis." I never lie about having done an analysis. But I will admit sometimes I am aware that if I do an analysis, I might not *like* the results, so I don't want to know.

Not having all of the facts at your fingertips can sometimes be an advantage because it gives you time to think. When I was starting out in the energy industry, I supported my boss when he was a witness but I was not the witness myself. His title and position at the company gave him more credibility than I had, even though I did all the actual work and analysis which was, frankly, outside of his expertise. (This is more common in cases involving corporations than you might think.) However, my boss was an engineer; I was the statistical expert. When he was on the witness stand, he specifically told me to take a vacation day. That way, if the opposing side asked a question he wasn't prepared for, he could say, "I'll have to check with my staff on that." Since I would not be available to answer the phone, he was guaranteed time to think about how to phrase the answer. Keep in mind this was before the age of smart phones. Today he would probably have advised me to turn off my company cellphone or leave it at the office.

NOTES ON ALWAYS TELL THE TRUTH

_____

_____

_____

_____

_____

_____

_____

_____

_____

_____

_____

_____

_____

_____

_____

_____

NOTES ON ALWAYS TELL THE TRUTH (cont)

4. Remember That Although You Swear To Tell "The Truth, The Whole Truth, And Nothing But The Truth," It Is Impossible To Tell "The Whole Truth" And The Court Won't Actually Let You

In most courtroom dramas, the witness stands with his hand on the bible and is asked, "Do you swear to tell the truth, the whole truth, and nothing but the truth, so help you God?"

And the witness answers, "I do"

However, many witnesses these days may be atheists, Buddhists, Muslims, etc. There are some Jews who interpret the command about "use the name of the Lord in vain" to include "unnecessary" or "trivial matters" and may object to swearing for some "less important" proceedings and not in others. Therefore, witnesses are commonly asked if they want to be sworn in or "affirmed." ("Do you affirm that the testimony you are about to give will be the truth, the whole truth, and nothing but the truth.") Note that some judges may have other variants. All these variants are legally binding and false testimony under any of them is a serious criminal matter.

While you must not lie, the reality is that you don't have to tell "the whole truth." In fact, the lawyer for the other side will frequently stop you from doing so. In theory, the point is to avoid wasting the court's time. In reality, the point is often to manipulate and control what the jury hears.

You may hear objections like:

a. *Relevance* – The contention that the information you want to give is not relevant to the case. This might be legitimately because you are rambling on about unimportant matters or it might be that the opposing lawyer feels the information you are giving could be distracting to the point *he* wants to be in the jury's mind.

b. *Non-responsive* – A lawyer usually asks specific questions to make a specific point. If your answer goes beyond what they asked for in their question (even if you think it is relevant) they may suggest your answer is not responsive to the question they actually asked. They may have part or all of it stricken from the record (and, therefore, the judge or jury should ignore it when making their decision).

c. *Conjecture* or *lay opinion* – Something may seem to you an obvious conclusion from the information you have. For instance, if you see a man with a bloody knife standing over a dead body, it may seem obvious to you that he killed the victim. However, you do not actually know that; it is a guess. You may reach a conclusion that an expert on the matter might or might not agree with. However, since you are a layman, it is only a lay opinion, not an expert opinion. In one divorce case I know of, the wife's accountant tried to testify that the family home was worth more than the husband's side stated. Since the accountant was not an expert in housing appraisals, the accountant's estimate was thrown out.

Note that this may not be the end of the matter. Your lawyer will get a turn to ask you follow-up questions "on redirect" (or "recross"). In any of these cases, make a note of what you wanted to say. As an expert, I take written notes, but check with your lawyer about how he thinks that would be perceived by the judge and jury. During the break, share those notes with your lawyer. He may decide the matter is not important or he may decide to ask you to give the full answer which will help to undermine the point the opposing lawyer was trying to make.

NOTES ON THE TRUTH, THE WHOLE TRUTH AND NOTHING BUT...

NOTES ON THE TRUTH, THE WHOLE TRUTH, AND NOTHING BUT... (cont)

5.   Keep A Cool Head

If you get angry or upset, it becomes easier—not harder—for the opposing lawyer to take advantage of you. It then becomes more likely you will forget the details and facts you worked out with your lawyer to help your case. Let's face it, when a person gets mad, others tend to assume that person has something to hide.

I said initially the courtroom is theatre and it is. But you can (and should) also think of it as a game—a game with rules. I like to think the game is biased in favor of the good guys, truth and justice, but it is still a game nevertheless. The better you play the game, the better your side has a chance of winning.

Personally, I am a game player. I like playing games and I like winning. I always bring the attitude that it is a game and fun to be on the witness stand. Playing a game well requires a cool head and attention to detail. If you get too upset about the possibility of losing, you'll lose concentration and make mistakes. If you get too excited about the possibility of winning, the same thing will happen.

Most importantly, think about what you are saying, what you need to say and what you need to avoid saying. Many of the points in the following sections will fundamentally be suggestions on how to do this and how to do it well.

NOTES ON KEEPING A COOL HEAD

NOTES ON KEEPING A COOL HEAD (cont)

6.   Keep In Mind That Most Cases Involve Legitimate Differences Of Opinion Between Men Of Good Will

I am not going to tell you that if you just tell the truth and stick to the facts everything will be fine. But I will tell you that, for the most part, the people on the other side are not fundamentally bad people. They have a different perspective than you do. They saw (or see) things differently than you do but, in general, do not assume they are lying or evil. There are some bad folks out there—and you might even know some—but most of them are not. Some folks are aggressive in "defending" their position (ask yourself if you are one of them) and that may make you uncomfortable (which is one of the reasons they get aggressive). Generally speaking, though, they are not evil. More importantly, it does you no good to assume they are evil.

If you think of them not as lying but as having a different perspective or being misguided or uninformed, you can keep a cooler head. If you think they are trying their best and that you simply need to educate and correct them, you will be far better equipped to sway the judge in your favor. Never forget that swaying the judge and jury are your goals, not persuading the opposing lawyer and witnesses.

Also remember that "He is a bald-faced liar!" isn't a very persuasive argument. It doesn't prove anything; it doesn't contain any facts which will make the judge or jury decide you are the one who should be believed. Even if your opponent *is* a bald-faced liar, the jury needs something concrete besides the strength of your beliefs.

However, "He is incorrect, although he believes ... that is not consistent with the following facts..." arguments will make the judge and jury take notice if you follow them up with an explanation of why.

Similarly, if you think an opposing lawyer or witness is misguided or mistaken (rather than lying), you are in a better mindset to understand why they have the mistaken view they do. This makes it easier to argue against it, perhaps when you are on the stand, perhaps when you are explaining things to your lawyer for his closing arguments and briefs afterwards. This advice goes hand-in-hand with the advice in Chapter 8: "Find all the weaknesses in your story before the opposition does and know how to respond." If you think about the weaknesses in your arguments, you will have thought about how someone could be led to believe them. This will put you in a better mindset to talk the judge and jury out of believing it than if you think the only reason someone could question your testimony is because they are dishonest.

You should also be aware that the opposing witnesses and lawyers want a different outcome than you do. You, obviously, want the best outcome for your side. They want the best outcome for their side. This means they will (both consciously and subconsciously) pick the facts or beliefs which support their side. You are doing exactly same thing. Your ultimate goal is to convince the judge and/or jury that what is right for your side is best for everyone who is affected.

NOTES ON LEGITIMATE DIFFERENCES OF OPINION

NOTES ON LEGITIMATE DIFFERENCES OF OPINION (cont)

7. Figure Out What Story You Want To Tell And Practice Telling It

Giving a sales presentation takes practice and forethought. So does making a presentation to the big boss. Like these presentations, an appearance on the witness stand is a chance to make your case before decision makers. The same basic rules of preparation apply. You want the decision makers to know what is in it for them if they accept what you are offering, and you want them to believe they will get it, whether it is profits from a sale or the feeling of having made the right decision and having done justice.

As I've said earlier, one of the worst pieces of advice to a witness is, "Just tell the truth and everything will be fine." Telling the truth is important, *very* important. But how you tell the truth, your posture, confidence and emphasis are also important. Remember, it is possible to tell the truth in a way that will not lead people to believing it *is* the truth. That is *not* the way you want to tell it.

You should remember that your real goal is not to get the judge and jury to believe you. It is to get them to believe *what you are saying*. While believing in you may go a long way, getting them to reach the same conclusion on their own goes even further. If you tell them your opinion, they can believe you or not believe you. But if you can get them to believe your story and can get it to make sense to them, that is even better. If, based on what they hear, they reach the same conclusion as you did, they will have a *commitment* to what you are telling them. That is what you need to cement your testimony in their hearts and minds. Lead them to make the right conclusion. Don't just tell them what it is.

If you want them to buy the whole story, never just "wing it" on the witness stand. Know what you want to say, know the key points you want to get across, and think about how everything you say will sound and be received. I am probably repeating what your lawyer has already told you.

Before you go on the witness stand, ask yourself what you want the jury to hear and remember. Ask yourself how you are going to take them from not knowing anything (or, in some cases, knowing what the other side has said) to knowing and believing what you want them to believe. This means they have to follow what you are telling them, follow the details, the flow and the logic. They don't just want to be *told*, they want to *understand*. Remember that the other side will probably tell a different version of the same events, or (in the case of experts) a different theory about what would have happened and what will happen under given circumstances.

When you are on the witness stand, remember that you want to give them a clear picture of what you saw, did or believe, and why. You want them to buy into your testimony with their minds and hearts.

Knowing your story also means knowing how to tell it when the other side asks questions about it. After all, they do not want the judge and jury to reach the same conclusions that your side does. They are going to ask questions about your version of the truth. Be prepared for those questions.

Learn from politicians. They get asked questions by the media all the time. They always come back to their "talking points." While they cannot afford to be obviously evasive, they consistently turn each question to the point or points they want to emphasize. You want to do the same thing. Instead of just answering the question the opposing lawyer asks, think about how to turn the response to what you want to say, to what you want to leave the judge and jury with.

Although this book is about being on the witness stand, a slight digression is called for at this point. There are actually three ways to testify: written testimony, depositions and from the witness stand itself. Usually, before any of these occur, there is some sort of discovery process. Most of the advice in this book is applicable to all three forms of discovery and to the discovery process.

Before Any Testimony Begins:

In many cases, before lawyers begin to develop a case, they will conduct "discovery." This is a process for collecting information. In criminal cases, it might be the list of witnesses, evidence list, forensic reports, etc. In civil cases, there might be a request for documents, etc. which could be used in making a case. Regulatory proceedings might sometimes ask that a study be done using data which only the company has. While anything which has been revealed during the discovery process can be used as evidence, there probably is a lot of information which is not useful.

As a professional witness, I am usually the one who asks the vast majority of the discovery questions.

I consult with my lawyer before anything goes out. We carefully go over the wording on any request so the opposing side cannot refuse to answer our questions based on a technicality or give us the data in some form which is not useful. Most of the things I am looking for to do my own analysis may have to come from the data I get from the opposing side. I will admit a significant portion of the data requests I submit I only glance at briefly. Sometimes the fact they have done a study tells me everything I want to know or, conversely, the fact they have *not* done a study may. There are some questions I ask to confirm what I already believe. There are a few I avoid asking because I don't want to tip off a third party to a proceeding as to what my thinking is, but that is rare. Surprises don't usually win cases, despite what you see on television.

Depositions:

A deposition is a meeting between a witness and his lawyers and the lawyers for the other side. It doesn't take place at a courthouse; usually they are in corporate offices or one of the lawyer's offices. There is no judge in attendance: just a court reporter (a stenographer), the witness, the lawyers, and maybe some folks assisting the lawyers. Despite the informality, the witness is giving answers under oath and anything they say can be used in court later although it does not have to be. These depositions are really part of the discovery process; the courtroom appearances are possible later.

In a deposition, the lawyers can ask their questions. Although your lawyer can object to a question, you should still answer it. If the question comes up in court, the judge will review the objection and may sustain (agree with) it. However, if you do not answer and the judge does not sustain the objection, there may be heavy fines involved.

From the witness' point of view, there are some nice things about depositions. You don't have to worry about talking to the judge; he isn't there. The other thing is that the opposing lawyers may tip their hand in terms of what their case is going to look like, so you have extra "prep" time to figure out how to answer similar questions when you are actually on the witness stand.

Written Testimony:

Sometimes witnesses prepare written testimony in advance of any courtroom appearance.

This permits long and detailed narratives with lots of specifics and support. Not only is it often easier to read long testimony than it is to stay awake through long narratives on the stand, it is easier for the other side to absorb, ask questions about and respond to. Frequently, the other side, upon reading your testimony, will ask data requests like the discovery mentioned above. In some cases, the data requests may ask for further explanations of the testimony. These explanations could potentially be used in evidence, so the individuals preparing the documents need to be very careful to make sure any answers they give are correct and have been cleared by their lawyers. Written testimony may then be followed by written rebuttal testimony, more data requests, written surrebuttal testimony, and then ultimately by final testimony on the witness stand.

On the Witness Stand:

The final stage of testifying is on the witness stand. Even if you have participated in any or all of the other phases, this is when the opposing lawyers get to ask (or ask again) any or all of their questions and you get to rebut other parties' arguments.

The Next Step:

After all the witnesses are finished and all of the evidence is presented, the lawyers sum up. In a jury trial, this is done in closing arguments and in a "bench trial" (one where the judge makes the decisions) the lawyers may submit written briefs and then often respond to the other party's briefs in "reply briefs." For many witnesses, it is over by now. For some witnesses, it may still be a chance to help the lawyer, especially for expert technical witnesses who may have a better memory for some technical details than the lawyer, simply by virtue of the fact they are versed in the subject matter whereas the lawyer is versed in the law.

However, it is important for the witness to keep the end in mind. What will your lawyer have to say? When I am on the witness stand, I think about simple quotable lines for me to say which my lawyer can use in his summations. When the lawyer can quote a simple one-sentence answer it has power. If he has to try to distill several paragraphs of response into a sound bite it is harder for him.

In some ways, my work starts even earlier. I do my research, my analysis, and everything leading up to putting together testimony with the final summaries in mind. How will someone attack my testimony? How can I make sure that attack is weak? If I am questioning someone else's testimony, how can I make sure I have covered all of the bases. It may not be enough to have a "better" analysis. how can I show the weaknesses in the opposing testimony and in a way that it is easy for the lawyer to sum up?

As a side note, I also recommend strongly you make notes on everything you saw or say, everything you might want to say later, etc. For professionals, document every piece of information you can, including where you got it. I also put all of my calculations down in an Excel spreadsheet so I have no problem remembering exactly how I got any number. When you do a calculation, do as few calculations in your head as possible. Make sure you write down the formulas. You will be amazed at how often an "obvious" calculation ceases to be obvious to you. Once you put a calculation in your testimony, if the opposition asks how you got it, it isn't enough to come up with a close number; you need to be able to tell them exactly how you got it (and why you used that particular formula) so make it as easy to replicate it as possible.

I also make copious notes about where my information comes from, how good it is, and any possible weaknesses. However, whenever I have potential weaknesses, I put them in a written document which I share with my lawyer. That way, the document is protected by "Attorney/Client privilege" (and should be marked as such). Otherwise, the opposing side could subpoena my notes and use the information against us in court.

Most of the cases I work on are primarily based on written testimony so I put a lot of footnotes, citing the data request, news article, web page, etc. where I got a piece of information. As an economic witness, I frequently cite economic principles and will make a note of a book (and page) where I can find this principle documented so the judge knows it is not just my pet theory. This not only avoids questions about my facts, it establishes my credibility when I am writing the testimony in the first place.

If you are not writing your testimony, it still is in your best interest to take copious notes. These notes may include sources. For example, what company memo are you quoting and where is it in the files in case you need to produce it later in the process. It might also include related observations such as "Even though it was dark, I remember there were four streetlights, one of which was out, but three were working."

Some witnesses, especially professionals, are normally expected to have notes. As an expert, I always go up on the stand with a notebook or two full of notes. I would expect members of law enforcement to have notes as well but, realistically, anyone can bring up notes.

That said, I always realize any notes I bring with me can, in theory, be asked for by the opposing lawyer. I have never had a lawyer ask for my whole notebook, but they have asked for the particular page I am reading from. For that reason, I don't just scrawl my notes, and I keep my "negative" notes and comments (those which might expose any questions or concerns I have about my testimony) on, at a minimum, a separate sheet of paper and usually attach a counter argument to that paper as well. I will often rewrite my notes up as "exhibits." That way, if an opposing lawyer wants to see the note, I can easily pass a copy to my lawyer and the judge and it is easy and (if I have done it right) convincing to the judge and jury when they look at it.

NOTES ON YOUR STORY

NOTES ON YOUR STORY (cont)

_____

_____

_____

_____

_____

_____

_____

_____

_____

_____

_____

_____

_____

_____

_____

_____

8.   Find All The Weaknesses In Your Story Before The Opposition Does And Know How To Respond

The reality is that no one's story is perfect. If you think yours is, think again. The opposing lawyer will make every effort to poke holes in your testimony. Depending upon the type of testimony you are offering, they might suggest that something might have blocked your vision, something someone said might have meant something else, aren't there other theories, or what if the data were flawed?

As much as possible, you want to avoid being surprised by these challenges. You want to have an answer to each of them before you appear on the stand. Done properly, this can be amazingly effective. First of all, it makes you look very confident and competent. The opposing lawyer would love to throw you off guard. If he can't, he never gets control. It can make him look like he is flailing wildly looking for something (which will put him off guard), and it definitely makes him violate his number one rule, "Never ask a question you don't know the answer to."

It also has an infectious effect on the jury. If you have thought through all of the possible problems and have a ready answer, you are more confident and that means they feel confident in believing in you. If you practice this in advance, you can come off as a confident expert, not as a smart aleck.

Many witness who master this find that the opposing lawyers don't ask them any questions at all after a while. In fact, I've seen one or two who do more damage to the opposing case when being cross-examined because they have answers (sometimes wonderfully folksy answers). I recall one witness who was asked about who owned the gas pipeline leading to a house—the gas company or the home owner. The witness responded by talking about selling his own home and then discovering he could not take the drapes with him. His answer was so comfortable and so convincing, even though it didn't actually deal with gas pipelines, that at the break afterwards, I could hear the lawyers cursing themselves out for having asked the question, and vowing never to ask him another one.

NOTES ON THE WEAKNESSES IN YOUR STORY

NOTES ON YOUR STORY (cont)

_____

_____

_____

_____

_____

_____

_____

_____

_____

_____

_____

_____

_____

_____

9.   Think Before Answering Any Question

When someone asks you a question, do not answer too quickly. They have a reason for the question and that reason is not because they are curious. Far from it. They want you to give them something they can use. Sometimes it is something to affect the jury immediately, sometimes it is something they will want to use to make you look good (if it is your lawyer) or bad (if it is the opposing lawyer.) Each piece of information is a chance to shine or a trap. In either case, you want to be aware and careful.

What are the assumptions hidden in the question? Are they reasonable? Sometimes, taking a question at face value is letting the opposing lawyer slip something in. Often, something you would not want to say if you thought about it is hard to go back once you've accepted it. (I will talk more about this in the next chapter.)

For the professional witness, there is no greater example of this danger than the "hypothetical question." The opposing lawyer may identify a question as a hypothetical one, admitting in advance that the question assumes facts not yet established in court. This may be because he is planning on putting these facts on the record later, or it may be because he wants to show the judge and jury that the story he is trying to tell is reasonable. I always specify very clearly the conditions that I am "accepting" in my answer and challenge, if appropriate, the reasonableness of the assumptions.

Thinking also gives you a chance to look intelligent and careful. If you answer without thinking and later have to revise your answer, you don't look as reliable. This is especially true if you follow the advice in the chapter about educating the judge and jury. Thinking gives you a chance to figure out how to say something so the judge and jury will understand and believe it.

NOTES ON THINKING BEFORE ANSWERING

NOTES ON THINKING BEFORE ANSWERING (cont)

_____

_____

_____

_____

_____

_____

_____

_____

_____

_____

_____

_____

_____

_____

10. Figure Out What The Opposing Lawyer Wants You To Say … And Then Do Not Say It. And, When In Doubt, Don't Say Anything!

It is better to be thought a fool, than to speak and remove all doubt.

- Attributed to Abraham Lincoln

A good lawyer never asks a question they don't already know the answer to. Or at least, that is their plan. One of my secrets to being a good witness is keeping the opposing lawyer from knowing the answer I am going to give.

Not saying what the opposing lawyer wants you to say does not mean not telling the truth. You should *always* tell the truth. But how you say what you say can vary a great deal without in any way endangering the truth. For example, perhaps you want to say, "I would not put it that way, but I guess it is *technically* correct." Or you might want to put an explanation or a spin on your answer which includes information the opposition would just as soon not have on the record and certainly would prefer not be in the jury's mind.

My very first time on the witness stand, the opposing lawyer wanted to make a point about the benefits of having more observations for a statistical analysis. He started out by asking me if I had a calculator with me. I did.

"I would like you," he said, "to take the average of two numbers; zero and 100."

Playing along, I entered both numbers into my calculator and got the average (50) and then said, "Let me double-check my numbers. Would you accept the answer to one decimal place?" He agreed. I replied, "50 point zero."

At this point, I had established I was playful and cooperative and the judge was mildly amused.

Then he said, "Now, I would like you to take the average of these eight numbers: 57, 16, 0, 93, 86, 100, 91, 77."

I punched in the numbers and did my calculations. I double-checked and confirmed my numbers. Then, I threw him a curve, "Would you like the arithmetic average or the geometric average?"

A mild look of panic came into his eyes. Not being a mathematician, he had no idea what the difference was or which (if either) of the two he wanted. He looked around for someone in his entourage to help him. They muttered and conferred, looking for someone who had the slightest idea what I was talking about. Eventually, one of the more minor witnesses on his side realized what I was talking about and told him.

"The arithmetic average will be fine."

I gave it to him. But, he quickly moved on to the next subject in his list. He completely dropped the subject. If I had given him the arithmetic average,[1] he would have gone on, but he was so flustered (and afraid of what math might come at him next) that he completely lost his train of thought. Don't get me wrong, I knew all along what he wanted; I just was determined not to give it to him.

Being on the witness stand can be a lot like playing a game. When one plays chess, one does not

---

[1]

This is what most people mean by average. It's the sum of the numbers divided by the number of them, in this case, the sum, 520 divided by 8, which comes to 65. The geometric average is determined by multiplying all of the numbers together and then figuring what number, multiplied by itself (eight times) would result in that same number. Since one of the numbers here was zero, the answer would have been zero.

just think about the most recent move the opponent made. One thinks about the moves he is going to make. Each move or series of moves is part of a long-term plan. When you are on the witness stand, you want to be a game player, too. The same rule about thinking three or four moves ahead (at least) applies to how you want to answer a question. The opposing lawyer has a game plan. He may be setting you up to go in one direction where he has a "trap" laid for you. The trick is to not stay on that path so that, by the time he gets to the third question, he has completely failed in laying the foundation he wanted to lay.

You should also remember there are two times you get to respond to a question. The first is when it is asked. The second is after the opposing lawyer is finished with all their questions when your lawyer can ask you for a "clarification" of a response you tried to give, in what is called "redirect." Even if the opposing lawyer objects to part of your answer as "non-responsive" (i.e., "That isn't what I asked") a complete answer on your part tells your lawyer what you want to include. You lawyer can only ask questions on redirect about things which were discussed in your opponent's cross-examination. If you brought up something—even if the opposing lawyer tries to dismiss it—it is usually fully admissible.

NOTES ON NOT SAYING WHAT THE OPPOSING LAWYER WANTS YOU TO

_____

_____

_____

_____

_____

_____

_____

_____

_____

_____

_____

_____

_____

_____

NOTES ON NOT SAYING WHAT THE OPPOSING LAWYER WANTS YOU TO (cont)

11. The Opposing Lawyer Is Not Your Friend And He Is Not The One You Have To Convince

Remember who is making the decision in the case. It isn't the lawyers; it is the judge and/or jury. Never lose sight of that reality.

We are naturally motivated to try to get people to like and believe us. Since we are talking to the lawyer, we naturally want the opposing lawyer to be our friend. A good lawyer ("good", as in "good at their job", not "good" as in "he's a good guy, you can trust him") can take advantage of this in one of two ways.

Some lawyers try a friendly approach, and it puts the witness off his guard. They know what they want you to say and then set you up to give them the answer they want because … well, because you want them to like you and instinctively cooperate with them as you do with any friend. Remember what I said in the last chapter: "Figure out what the opposing lawyer wants you to say and then do not say it." Never lose sight of the fact you don't care about the opposing lawyer's approval; you want the judge and jury to buy into your version of the facts.

Some lawyers use a slightly different approach; they will appear reasonable but skeptical. Their intention is to make witnesses feel needy. The result is often that the witnesses get a little confused by the fact the opposing lawyer does not accept their story and they tend to say too much, which makes them vulnerable to challenges later. The witnesses say too much and may make mistakes or reveal weaknesses in their testimony.

In both of these cases, the witnesses have—in an attempt to be helpful to the opposing lawyer—violated a basic rule; they stop telling the story they've practiced.

During my divorce, I spent a fair amount of time on the witness stand. At one break, my own lawyer said, "You are doing great, but I can't quite figure out what you are doing."

I responded, "Have you noticed my wife's lawyer tends to make mistakes when she gets angry?"

"Yes."

"What I am doing is annoying her, subtly, so the judge won't notice and object."

"Well, it is working wonderfully. Keep it up!"

I did, and the divorce case went substantially my way. This is a technique which one has to be very careful and very skillful about using. I do not recommend it for the inexperienced witness. Even for those who know how to do it, it should be done very sparingly. Why? If the judge objects, you are likely to be admonished, and that does not look good.

NOTES ON THE OPPOSING LAWYER

NOTES ON THE OPPOSING LAWYER (cont)

12.   Look The Judge And Jury In The Eye

Credibility is often about perception. If you look and sound like a person who is telling the truth and if you look and sound like someone who believes what they are saying, the judge and jury are more likely to believe it, too.

Start by talking to the judge and jury, not the lawyer asking the questions. This may seem a little awkward at first. After all, you are answering the lawyer's questions but it really isn't the lawyer you want to believe you. It is the judge and jury. This same rule applies whether you are answering your lawyer's questions or you are answering the questions of the opposing lawyer. Note that making eye contact with the judge and jury also helps you to avoid the natural urge to be a "friend" to the opposing lawyer.

Dishonest people tend to avoid eye contact. We tend, as a result, to distrust people who avoid eye contact and to trust people who look us straight in the eye. But eye contact is more than just about honesty, per se. We feel connected with people who we make eye contact with. Eyes show our intentions. They move in conjunction with the use of our right and left brain activity. This tells the person we are making contact with if we are thinking about what we are saying or simply instinctively telling what we believe to be the truth.

Eye contact can actually trigger the release of Oxytocin, the chemical associated with mother/child bonding (and also with the bond between humans and dogs, by the way). It has the same effect between a witness and a member of the jury. It bonds us and creates trust by associating our words with an "emotional truth."

We should, however, make eye contact in moderation. If we stare at someone, it makes them feel uncomfortable; it is simply too much intimacy. Keep the amount of time you make eye contact to a comfortable level but definitely make it, especially when making the points you most want them to absorb and remember.

At the same time as you are making eye contact, you want to display the other aspects of confidence. Speak in a calm and reassuring manner. (This is why I am professorial.) If you are too aggressive, it associates your words with a negative and uncomfortable emotional response for the judge and jury. This is not how you want them to react. If you sound too tentative, your lack of certainty is what they will remember. This is why, even though I could hold my own in an out-and-out argument, I try for a professorial approach. I am calm, confident, in control, and pleasant. These are the emotions the judge and jury associate with my testimony, which is exactly what I want.

The other advantage of making eye contact is that it lets you know how the person hearing you is reacting to your words. Do they look puzzled? If so, you need to explain a little more clearly. Do they look bored (or, worse yet, hostile)? If so, you should move on to another point. And so on.

Eye contact with the person or persons you want to convince can go a long way to making them like you and believe you. Never forget it is the judge and jury you want to convince.

NOTES ON LOOK THE JUDGE AND JURY IN THE EYE

_____

_____

_____

_____

_____

_____

_____

_____

_____

_____

_____

_____

_____

_____

_____

_____

NOTES ON LOOK THE JUDGE AND JURY IN THE EYE (cont)

13. Teach The Judge And Jury, Don't Just Tell Them

While appealing to the emotions of the judge and jury is obviously important, that won't do the whole trick. After all, even if they like you, they know you could be wrong. You have to get them emotionally invested in your version of the facts.

The idea is that everything you say should make sense to the judge and jury. They should feel what you felt when you saw something, they should understand why you did whatever you did. If you are explaining why you believe something to be true, they should understand the logic.

It is important, therefore, to think like a storyteller. Start your testimony from the beginning, build the story with logic (and, to some degree, drama) until it reaches a logical conclusion. You want your version of the story to take root in their consciousness. If you just tell them something, it only lies on the surface, and—like something laying on the ground—it is easy to pick up, move or throw out. However, if you *teach* them something, it takes root, and it is much harder to dislodge.

You want them intellectually and emotionally invested in your story. If a lawyer or another witness contradicts you, the judge and jury should feel uncomfortable with the opposing version of the story. They have seen, heard and thought through things the way you do. It is harder for them to doubt you if they understand and accept logically and emotionally what you've told them. When the opposition tries to convince them of something else, the judge and jury should be "invested" in your version of events. Accepting someone else's version should (if you, as a witness, have done your job right) make the jury uncomfortable because it will contradict what they have accepted at a deeper level.

NOTES ON TEACHING NOT JUST TELLING

NOTES ON TEACHING NOT JUST TELLING (cont)

---

14.   Remember "The Law Guarantees Everyone A Fair Trial, Nothing Can Guarantee Them A Fair Decision"

My grandfather was a civil rights attorney in Alabama in the 1930s. He believed in the law and he believed in equality. Judges and jury members, though, are human. They come with their own set of prejudices and preconceived notions. They come with blinders. Everyone does. Realistically, you have to accept that.

As powerful as the image of a civil rights trial in 1930s Alabama is, the same reality fundamentally holds true today, although less dramatically. A friend of mine makes his living advising lawyers about jury selection. Who goes on the jury makes a difference. Why? Because decisions are not made by the facts; they are made by the people who hear the facts.

The secrets of selecting a jury are the subject for another book, but I will share with you what I was once told about my ever being selected as a juror. "It will never happen."

You see, lawyers want people on the jury that they can manipulate emotionally and intellectually.

Even before I became an expert witness, I was an economist, specializing in economic statistics. Lawyers do not want people who do their own analysis. Quite the opposite. The lawyer wants to do the analysis for the jury so the jury has to reach the conclusion he has in mind. Someone like me, who is used to thinking critically and looking for holes in an argument is not what he wants. Which means I am *not* a likely candidate to be selected for the jury box.

That's also why a "jury of your peers" seldom includes a lawyer. A lawyer in the jury box will recognize the tricks that the lawyers for the prosecution and defense (or plaintiff, etc., depending upon the kind of case) are using. Professional witnesses like myself also learn to recognize the tricks of the trade.

Sure enough, I have been called to jury duty many times. I would love to sit on a jury and do my civic duty. I have never made it through the *voir dire* (the jury selection process).

In addition to the importance of selecting the right jury, the outcome of the case will frequently depend upon who the judge is. It has been my experience that judges frequently have track records which show they have a liberal or conservative bias, sympathy for some arguments and a lack of sympathy for others. Some judges like to have as much evidence as possible on the record, trusting that the final decision makers can find the truth in it and reject the inappropriate facts or utterances. Others like to make sure that only the relevant evidence is admitted, to control the final decision and leave little room (based on the record) for any questions or challenges later. Some lawyers take the choice of a judge philosophically and they should. But, in any theatre, you want to know your audience, know what they like and don't like. and adapt your performance (testimony) accordingly.

Don't forget that judges, being human, have their own personal agendas just like the rest of us. They all want to enforce the law. They also want to go home at the end of the day and feel they made a difference. They hate to be reversed on appeals. Some even have political ambitions from re-election to appointment to a higher level of judgeship to election to a different office altogether.

Lastly, we all know that high power lawyers get to be high power lawyers for a reason. They have a better win/loss record than other lawyers. Let's be honest; they don't just pick the right cases, they know the techniques that tend to work in the court room.

According to a 2014 article by Samuel Gross in the Proceedings of the National Academy of Sciences approximately 4.1 percent of the convicted felons on death row were wrongly accused. That is roughly 1 in 25. That is where there is the strongest level of certainty. Convictions of a crime must be *beyond a reasonable doubt*. How many more errors of fact would be made in civil trials where the standard is the much lower *preponderance of the evidence* (i.e., where it only has to seem more likely to be true than to be false)?

Ultimately, the witness has to accept this is the reality. Denying it will only result in anger and ulcers. Be philosophical. The law is designed to protect the innocent, and judges and juries worry more about protecting the person or persons they see as the underdog. If you get angry about it, it will distract you from the bigger picture. Accept it, keep calm about it and move on.

NOTES ON FAIR TRIALS VS. FAIR DECISIONS

NOTES ON FAIR TRIALS VS. FAIR DECISIONS (cont)

_____

_____

_____

_____

_____

_____

_____

_____

_____

_____

_____

_____

_____

_____

_____

15.   Accept That The Law Is The Law

Although people talk about "justice," it is important to realize that the law and "right and wrong" are different things. That's just the way it is. When lawmakers write the laws, they can't possibly foresee every possibility. They may have written the laws with certain interests in mind. They may be biased in favor of the "little guy" or in favor of "protecting property." They may have a belief that it is in a child's best interest to be with its mother and write laws with biases in that direction. They may not have understood or predicted modern technology and just did the best they could.

It is your lawyer's job to figure out what the law says and help direct you towards saying the right things to make persuasive arguments under that law. Accept that. Any good speaker knows that you want to direct your arguments towards what people actually will do (in this case, what the law will *let* them do), not towards your personal ideal.

Sometimes the law is just stacked against you or your cause. Telling the judge "that isn't right" or "that isn't fair" won't help. The judge is obligated to uphold the law, whether *he* believes in it or not. Your lawyer may object to a particular ruling in the course of the case (and that is his place, not yours), or he may feel there is an adequate basis to appeal a ruling. Again, let him do that; as a witness, that is not your job.

If you are not too personally invested in a case, you can just chock up one to the win or loss column at the end of a case and hope for a good record. I realize that if you are invested in a case, it may be a lot tougher emotionally. Put your emotions aside when you are on the stand. The place to change the law is not on the witness stand. It isn't when the lawyer is summing up. The place to change the law is in the court of public opinion, in speeches before the civil groups and presentations to your elected representatives. On the witness stand, you have to keep your mind clear.

NOTES ON ACCEPTING THE LAW IS THE LAW

NOTES ON ACCEPTING THE LAW IS THE LAW (cont)

_____

_____

_____

_____

_____

_____

_____

_____

_____

_____

_____

_____

_____

_____

Final Thoughts

There are good witnesses and bad witnesses. There are comfortable witnesses and uncomfortable ones. There is no reason why you cannot be a good witness. There is no reason for you to be an uncomfortable one.

If you follow the tips in this book, stay calm, remember who you are trying to convince, look them in the eye and practice giving your testimony and preparing for the opposing lawyer's questions by seeking out (and practicing how to respond to) the weaknesses in your testimony, you won't win every case. The odds, however, will have shifted into your favor.

About the Author

Michael Alexander has a Ph.D. in Applied Economics from The University of Minnesota and has presented and supervised testimony in over 150 cases before the California and Minnesota Public Utility Commission and the Federal Energy Regulatory Commission.

As a witness and witness coach, he has won over $1.5 Billion worth of judgments and settlements for his clients.

Michael has also trained students for the competitive California Mock Trial Competition. His students have gone to the quarter or semi-finals for four years in a row. Several of his students have also won individual awards.

Michael Alexander has several programs to help you:

1. Survive and Thrive on the Witness Stand:

A basic hour long primer for witnesses

• Learn to present your case and be believable

• Understand the courtroom dynamics

• Take the fear out of the process

http://www.AlexanderTalks.com

2. Training Your Witnesses

An hour long (or optionally longer) CLE course

- Teach your witnesses to work with you not against you
- Make sure the record contains what you want it to
- Improve the relationship between you and your client

3. An Introduction to the Court for Witnesses & Spectators

An hour long introduction to general legal proceedings

- Take the mystery out of the legal process
- Gain a perspective when watching a trial you care about
- Understand more than just what the news and friends say

4. Individualized Coaching

A program customized to your case and your needs Michael is available to work with lawyers and witnesses to help maximize their comfort and probability of success in any courtroom appearances.

Contact him at Michael@AlexanderTalks.com

What Clients Say:

I had the fortune of observing Mike work with witnesses… It takes a unique aptitude to absorb complicated material and testify as a witness. Mike's exceptional talent is his ability to transcend that skill set and teach others to provide succinct and effective testimony in a courtroom setting.

- Jeff Renzi, Attorney

Michael is a consummate teacher, as demonstrated in his patience and skill in instructing middle-school students to excel in a mock trial competition. Michael is able to take complex problems and explain them in plain language that can be comprehended even by sixth graders.

- Allan Johnson, Attorney, Head Of EIX Ethics Investigations

Group

Michael's speech was both a mind-opener and a heart-opener to me. He helped me understand the things in ways I never would have without his help.

- Rev. Daniel Huston

Michael Alexander is a throw back to the days when society valued verbal communication. 'Dr. Mike' uses his wit, his vast knowledge, and his unique perspective on life to teach, to explain, and to humor anyone and everyone he communicates with.

- Rudy Fuentes, Montery Highlands' Teacher

I have known Dr. Michael Alexander more than twenty years, and have attended more than a dozen of his presentations. Dr. Alexander is always concise, and is able to make the most difficult problems clear. Besides being one of the world's foremost experts on the economics of energy, he is also a great story teller and showman.

- Stuart Goldbarg, Author, Jury Consultant

Made in the USA
Coppell, TX
07 September 2022

82763710R00069